ARCHITECTURE & DESIGN LIBRARY

ART NOUVEAU

ARCHITECTURE & DESIGN LIBRARY

ART NOUVEAU

Robert Fitzgerald

FRIEDMAN/FAIRFAX

PUBLISHERS

A FRIEDMAN/FAIRFAX BOOK

DP LS EX VRW C NS O6 TL JY DJ RW CADCC

© 1997 by Michael Friedman Publishing Group, Inc.

Library of Congress Cataloging-in-Publication Data

Fitzgerald, Robert, 1971-
    Art Nouveau / by Robert Fitzgerald.
        p.   cm — (Architecture & design library)
    Includes index.
    ISBN 1-56799-454-7
    1. Decoration and ornament—Art nouveau. 2. Art nouveau
(Architecture) I. Title. II. Series: Architecture and design
library.
    NK 1380.F55   1997
    745.4'441—DC21   97-7240
                                                      CIP

Editor: Francine Hornberger
Art Director: Kevin Ullrich
Layout Design: Ruth Diamond
Photography Editor: Deidra Gorgos
Production Manager: Camille Lee

Color separations by Colourscan Overseas Co Pte Ltd.
Printed in Hong Kong by Midas Printing Ltd.

1 3 5 7 9 10 8 6 4 2

For bulk purchases and special sales, please contact:
Friedman/Fairfax Publishers
Attention: Sales Department
15 West 26th Street
New York, New York 10010
212/685-6610   FAX 212/685-1307

Visit our website:
http://www.metrobooks.com

To Carol

C o n t e n t s

INTRODUCTION

The 1890s was one of the most tumultuous decades in the history of art and design. Although the close of a century is often marked by a momentous sense of transition and renewal, the dawning of the twentieth century witnessed the creation of a completely new art form. The nineteenth century had seen a dramatic rise in the power of science and industry and the establishment of a rigid Victorian morality, but the tide would turn. The avant-garde reacted against the call of Progress and sallied forth into an era of decadence and creative whimsy. There was a desire for new art forms—not merely a divergence from earlier styles, but a negation of what came before. In this age of fashionable despair, the greatest achievement was to thwart artistic convention, to make it new.

The Art Nouveau movement was conceived in this artistic milieu, born in cities across Europe and the United States. It remains one of the most imaginative and intriguing styles in the history of design. Today Art Nouveau is found in houses and apartments around the world, prominent in the homes of art aficionados and laymen alike. While some love Art Nouveau for its historical and cultural richness, others simply like how it looks. Because of the incredible range and diversity of the style, Art Nouveau can be used to enhance just about any setting. Whether you are building a home from scratch or merely remodeling, selecting new carpet or buying a vase for flowers, Art Nouveau will bring an interesting dimension to home design and decorating.

Before pulling up the old carpet, however, you should try to understand what all those curlicued flourishes and oddly geometric designs are about. Art Nouveau maintains a prominent place in the history of art and design, and considered in its historical context, the style takes on a whole new meaning.

The Art Nouveau movement freed the artist from centuries of academic and historical tradition. Although the notion of completely abstract

OPPOSITE: *Civic structures like Joseph Olbrich's Secession House in Vienna led the way in spreading Art Nouveau across Europe. Many of the styles and techniques employed in such structures would later be applied to domestic dwellings.*

ABOVE: *Nature was merely a starting point for Art Nouveau designers. This glassed-in subway station entrance in Torino, Italy, shows just how abstracted natural forms would become. The iron whiplash curves in the windows are distinctly organic, yet they do not resemble any particular plant form. Even the sculpted cornerstones seem only vaguely organic, like mutant gargoyles.*

art was still years away, it was no longer essential for a design to be formal or representational to be appreciated. Art Nouveau artists were among the first to create "art for art's sake." Decorative elements, which were previously used only as embellishments eventually became art forms in themselves.

A major objective of Art Nouveau artists was to create a sense of unity in all the arts: painting, architecture, furniture, glass, carpets, silver, murals, china and so forth. Art Nouveau practitioners wanted to incorporate their art into every aspect of life. Each and every art form added to the grand scheme of instilling beauty in the world at large and none was perceived as more worthy than the others. In an effort to create a sense of unity and harmony in interior decoration and architecture, artists often worked in several different fields, becoming the Renaissance men and women of their generation.

The influence of the machine and mass industry had on society played a crucial role in the development of Art Nouveau. The social, economic, and political change brought by the Industrial Revolution had great repercussions in the art world, which perceived industry as both a boon and a bane to society. On one hand, industrial development at the turn of the century was synonymous with science, progress, and human advancement. On the other, the industrial age brought with it rampant mass production. The day of the artisan was feared to be over. Many artists, therefore, shunned the machine and created a fantasy world where craft and morality went hand in hand. This world was Art Nouveau.

These nineteenth-century artists retreated into the world of nature. Nature, of course, had been a source of inspiration for ages, but Art Nouveau would forever alter the way artists would look at their natural surroundings. The new aesthetic demanded more than just an accurate depiction of nature. Artists sought not to imitate nature, but to reinvent it with their own imagination, to re-create it through a highly developed sense of linear form. Over the course of several years, Art Nouveau would abstract the physical world almost beyond recognition.

ABOVE: *The Art Nouveau movement placed great emphasis on detail, and the Spanish architect Antonio Gaudí (1852-1926) was one of the most detail-oriented designers of his time. The roofline of Casa Batlló shows the sublime quality of his work. High above the awestruck masses, Gaudí's architecture employs jewellike tiles and gilded arabesques to accent a mosaic façade. A serpentine roof and elfin spire top off the masterpiece.*

Nature provided the curvilinear motifs, but the artist produced the beauty and fantasy of Art Nouveau.

The series of international styles we now call Art Nouveau were known by several different names in Europe at the turn of the century. Several of these names refer to specific artists who championed the style in certain regions of Europe, while others allude to the style's decorative features. But whether it was called *Jugendstil* in Germany, *Le Style Moderne* in France, *Sezession* in Austria, *Stile Liberty* in Italy, *Modernista* in Spain, or *Style Horta* in Belgium, these disparate movements had much in common. Each region has its own distinctive look, but they are all petals of the same flower.

More than any other individual, William Morris (1834–96) was crucial in the development of Art Nouveau. Morris saw industry as the mortal enemy of art and design. For him, all aspects of design were equally important in creating beauty. Together with the influential art critic John Ruskin (1819–1900), Morris spearheaded the Arts and Crafts movement in England, which, in turn, led to the Art Nouveau movement. A master designer of furniture, glassware, and, most importantly, textiles, Morris' floral-patterned embroideries, wallpapers, and carpets are commonplace to this day. The Morris Company debuted his hand-crafted wares at the International Exhibition in London in 1862 and quickly achieved renown.

At the same Exhibition, interestingly, Japanese arts were shown for the first time in Europe. Almost overnight, Japanese objets d'art became the rage. The Japanese principles of composition and structure greatly influenced fine and decorative arts in England and, eventually, throughout Europe. The master of japonism was James McNeil Whistler (1834–1903), whose work would have profound influence on the Art Nouveau movement.

Despite the momentous precedent set in Great Britain during the nineteenth century, Art Nouveau never achieved the degree of adventurousness in England that it did in other European countries like Belgium and France.

The pages of this book will provide an overview of Art Nouveau design. After describing what characterizes the style, it will demonstrate how Art Nouveau design is applied to the contemporary home. Architecture, interiors, furniture, objets d'art, and accessories typical of this period will be presented to inspire you to use this fascinating style in your home.

LEFT: *The wallpaper in this antique-style dining area is based on a William Morris print and serves to brighten the otherwise subdued space. It is a wonderful example of how just one Art Nouveau component can change the feel of an entire room.*

ABOVE: *This living room contains a wealth of William Morris–designed textiles and furnishings. The carpet and throw pillows, for example, are all richly woven in bright colors. They have the intricate floral patterns for which Morris was well known. The wallpaper and curtains form a more subtle ensemble of muted green and the ceramic plate above the mantel is yet another Morris classic.*

CHAPTER ONE

ARCHITECTURE

A rt Nouveau architecture is demanding, to say the least. Even the original Art Nouveau practitioners had a difficult time applying what began as a two-dimensional decorative style to three-dimensional volumes. For those considering moving into or building an Art Nouveau house, be warned that it's a tricky style to master.

Even more than in the decorative arts, Art Nouveau architecture had to take a universal approach to design. Every detail and every design element had to conform to an all-encompassing artistic vision. The only way the architecture could succeed in maintaining its linear rhythms was if all exterior and interior design elements—from doors and windows to carpets and furnishings—blended cohesively. Thus, the exterior of an Art Nouveau structure often mirrors the interior.

The meticulous attention to detail eventually made Art Nouveau impracticable as an architectural style. Designing buildings in which every room, every piece of furniture, and every detail had to be coordinated demanded an enormous amount of time and money. In short, the architectural style was very impractical and could not sustain itself for long. It exploded on the European stage in a flurry and just as quickly disappeared, but left behind some of the most remarkable buildings the world will ever see.

In building an Art Nouveau–style building today, it is important to look back to the best Art Nouveau designers, those who embraced the movement's spirit and created buildings that not only looked but also felt organic, both inside and out.

The French architect Eugène Viollet-Le-Duc (1814–79) was largely responsible for bridging nineteenth-century Gothic Revival with Art Nouveau. A prolific restorer of medieval cathedrals, Viollet-Le-Duc pioneered the undisguised use of iron in architecture. He evolved a style of ornament that was consistent with the material and the structural demands of buildings, and his work was crucial to architects like Antonio Gaudí in Spain, Hector Guimard (1867–1942) in France, and Victor Horta (1861–1947) in Belgium—all of whom would become famous as leaders of Art Nouveau.

The architecture that emerged out of Glasgow and Vienna, on the other hand, represents another strain in the movement altogether. The

OPPOSITE: *This ornately carved façade is typical of Art Nouveau found in Eastern Europe, most notably in Prague and Vienna, where architectural decoration was simplified and much less flamboyant than in the West. Classical sculptures and friezes molded in high relief give this building a regal air.*

linear quality here suggests not flowing curves, but straight lines and rectilinear grids. While the two styles are certainly not exclusive, they do illustrate the wide variety of Art Nouveau aesthetics.

Antonio Gaudí was one of the most innovative architects the world has ever known. While Gaudí's early works were clearly inspired by the Hispano-Moorish architecture common to his native Barcelona, he quickly developed an inimitable style that—even today—is advanced both visually and technically. Gaudí's buildings are remarkable for their undulating surfaces, which appear not only surreal, but even illogical. The irony is that all of Gaudí's fantastic designs depend on a highly sophisticated understanding of both materials and engineering. The eccentric architecture of his Palacio Güell and Casa Batlló, for example, is the stuff of dreams, yet both designs are supported by remarkably sound engineering principles. A lofty pinnacle of Art Nouveau fantasy and invention, Gaudí's work demonstrates just how far the imagination can reach.

Another architect who employed vast imagination as well as rigorous intellect is Hector Guimard, one of the most accomplished architects of his day. Like Gaudí's work, Guimard's architecture has a highly organic quality derived from abstracted nature as well as Celtic motifs. The Castel Béranger is his pièce de résistance. Built in Paris in 1898, this apartment complex is at once whimsical and a highly refined synthesis of form and function. No detail escaped the architect's eye: the linear motifs on the light switches are the same as those that play along doorways and windowsills throughout the building.

Victor Horta's 1893 design for the Belgian Tassel House is considered one of the earliest—and finest—examples of High Art Nouveau. Horta was largely responsible for bringing to fruition some of the movement's most fantastic creations. His work is remarkable for its linear and decorative unity. Whiplash curves and arabesques dominate his architecture both inside and out, transforming mortar and steel into organic architecture.

Art Nouveau arrived late in Austria, and its influence there was confined almost entirely to Vienna. Nevertheless, the development of the movement in Vienna had enormous influence the rest of twentieth-century architecture and design. While Gustav Klimt is one of the most enduring artists from this period, the architects Joseph Olbrich and Josef Hoffmann had even greater sway over the shape of the world to come. Their work is notable for its monumental simplicity. In their creations, strong, simple volumes underscore the beauty of straight lines as well as the brilliant contradiction of spare curvilinear decoration.

ABOVE: *Gustav Klimt is one of the best-known artists of the Art Nouveau period. His painting,* The Kiss, *is among the most recognizable pieces from that time.*

ABOVE: *Art Nouveau architecture emphasizes designing all the elements of a space to produce a harmonious, coherent unity. The design process, therefore, often started on the inside and worked outward. Structural elements are incorporated into the architecture, their decorative possibilities exploited for the maximum effect.*

RIGHT: *Gaudí paid close attention to the textures of his buildings. He would often use several different types of masonry construction in a single project. Rock chips were used to form a mosaic pattern, as in this window-frame and pilaster. Carved stone was implemented for architectural details such as lintels.*

ABOVE: *Antonio Gaudí was one of the most inspired architects of his time—or any other, for that matter. These wrought-iron window gratings give a sense of Gaudí's enormous imagination. They are at once lyrically beautiful and darkly menacing. Gaudí's serpentine grillwork is juxtaposed against bright, colorful tiles and suggests the architect's playful sense of irony. The craftsmanship is of the highest caliber.*

OPPOSITE: *Gaudí's Casa Vicens is a spectacle to behold. While the crenelated window openings and iron palisades are fearsome and warlike, the effervescent tile façade appears capricious and comical. Only Gaudí could blend these two personalities so seamlessly in one structure.*

OPPOSITE and ABOVE: *The Art Nouveau movement even found its way to Mexico. This house adopts the flamboyant style of Belgian Art Nouveau designers. The wrought-iron fence surrounding the house mirrors the strange whiplash motifs found in the building's façade. The windows and balconies are remarkable for their peculiar parabolic shapes, as are the decorative friezes below the eaves.*

ABOVE: *More often than not, architectural peculiarities are integral facets within a larger design scheme. While this bulbous window and crowning brick arch appear quite anomalous and out of context, they in fact reinforce the building's organic design.*

RIGHT: *Art Nouveau architecture makes radically inventive use of iron and glass. Slender, articulated iron columns support large expanses of glass on this porch, imbuing the architecture with light and a sense of fluidity. The stained glass details extend the great decorative fantasy.*

ABOVE: *Even the more tame renditions of Art Nouveau architecture have certain unmistakable qualities. While this apartment building appears relatively simple, closer inspection reveals that every window has a beautifully carved stone lintel. The balconies are quite elaborate as well, and each has a sculpted iron railing that complements the architecture.*

LEFT: *As these balconies suggest, Art Nouveau can be quite capricious. These iron lattice railings and window mullions are fantastically designed, yet a certain symmetry lies beneath the cavorting spirals and arabesques that serves to unify the architecture.*

RIGHT: *This keyhole-shaped door is a classic example of Art Nouveau craftsmanship. Several different materials—leaded glass, sculpted wrought iron, carved wood, and masonry— are brought together in one complex design. In an earlier period, this may have been very difficult to achieve, but Art Nouveau designers prided themselves on their ability to master various mediums.*

LEFT: *With two carved busts standing sentry outside, this doorway seems almost like the entrance to an Egyptian tomb. Such mythic allusions occur frequently in Art Nouveau. The door's undulating mullions and glass panels lend a scaly, serpentine quality, demonstrating why glass is considered one of the most evocative mediums of Art Nouveau design.*

RIGHT: *In its most fanciful incarnations, Art Nouveau combines effervescent color with flamboyant design, ornate detail, and superb craftsmanship. This balcony and window certainly meet those requirements. While the Mediterranean palette gives this house a unique glow, the architecture is rather eye-catching as well. A rigorous imagination invented both the stained glass French doors and the bulbous wrought-iron railing.*

LEFT: *Viennese Art Nouveau features a dramatic interplay of structure and ornament. The most stoic and monumental architecture is often embellished with beautifully articulated floral designs. This building's bold lines and strong, flat planes are enhanced by a frieze that softens the effect of the architecture. The ornament is beautiful in itself, but it lends the building enormous depth.*

CHAPTER TWO

DESIGN FLOURISHES

Art Nouveau is at times difficult to define because it is made up of many distinct and diverse styles. While certain themes and characteristics appear throughout, it is important to remember that Art Nouveau is a means of personal, individual expression. The various styles of Art Nouveau, therefore, are as numerous as its creators.

Nevertheless, Art Nouveau's many maifestations can be traced to a common evolution. Across Europe and North America, turn-of-the-century artists reacted to their environments in similar ways. This is apparent in their work, which, however visually diverse, shares the same spirit of freedom and newness that greatly influenced the history of modern art.

Art Nouveau was inspired in many ways by the past that it loudly rejected. While Japanese and Gothic art were directly influential in the creation of Art Nouveau, other historical styles also played a significant role in the development of the style. Rococo art, with its elaborate ornamentation and fancifully curved asymmetry, certainly had a strong influence, as did the arabesque motifs of Moorish and Persian designs. William Morris championed the furniture designs of Tudor England, making that style a touchstone for Art Nouveau designers. The graphic design of Celtic manuscripts offered great inspiration as well. But Art Nouveau designers never tried to imitate their predecessors. They drew on the past and tried to make it new.

Art Nouveau forced a dramatic and fundamental change in the composition of art. A new sense of line and space allowed decorative motifs to gain autonomy. The whole perception of the line changed. Because the line was no longer restrained, the entire composition was free to pulse and undulate in new and imaginative ways. Lines were rendered and arranged for maximum beauty: spirals, waves, arabesques, whiplashes, and a variety of creeping tendrils became works of art in themselves.

Although Art Nouveau encompasses a sargasso sea of trends and styles, two basic tendencies emerge: curvilinear forms such as the whiplash and spiral, and rigid, rectilinear forms. When designing the home today, one typically is forced to choose between these two disparate tendencies. They often seem mutually exclusive in design schemes.

OPPOSITE: *Victor Horta's linear floral motifs became the hallmark of Art Nouveau design around the world. Wrought iron was one of Horta's favorite mediums, as shown in this curvaceous balustrade. Horta also used iron to shape the lighting fixtures and to frame the glass panels that appear throughout this house.*

The motif most often associated with Art Nouveau is based on the dynamic interplay of organic, curvilinear lines—the whiplash and spiral. In the history of modern art and architecture, this visual imagery stands out most spectacularly. These undulating, free-flowing designs are far different from anything that came before or after, and are therefore easily recognized. Most of Art Nouveau architecture and interior design today is created with this tendency in mind.

The other—issuing from Glasgow and Vienna—plays an even more important role in the development of modernism. While the interplay of lines is still the central means of expression, here the lines form rigid, tightly composed geometries remarkable for their spareness and efficiency of design. The examples on pages 54, 56 and 57 demonstrate this style of Art Nouveau most clearly. While quite diverse visually, both tendencies have much in common ideologically.

Abstracting the natural world allowed for remarkable freedom. Liberated from representational restraints, the artist was able to design anything he or she could imagine. Natural forms could be twisted, elongated, and curved to the spatial requirements of any composition. Flowers, birds, and the female form were favorite motifs. Slowly these motifs became more and more abstracted. In the Art Nouveau lexicon, these motifs converged into lines and sinuous curves without much differentiation. The ubiquitous *femme-fleur*, a design motif that is part woman, part flower, demonstrates this coming together. Eventually the style would become so abstract that whiplash curves and zigzag, S-shaped designs lost any correlation to the physical world. At that point, pure design was achieved.

The rhythmic forms of Art Nouveau have natural associations with music and dance, which became favorite motifs of the period as well. Art Nouveau championed the synthesis of all arts under one stylized aesthetic, and both music and dance could be easily applied to the two-dimensional designs of the period. The line pulsating with movement is the ultimate motif of the Art Nouveau style, and music and dance lend themselves to that method of expression remarkably well. In theory, too, Art Nouveau designs were linked to music, which has always been regarded as the purest art form. And purity, of course, was just what fin de siècle artists were after.

When designing and decorating the contemporary home in Art Nouveau, keep in mind its history of incorporating diverse influences. Some aspects of the style may seem vulgar to you, others sublime. The most satisfying experience in home design is discovering those pieces you find beautiful and intriguing and incorporating them into your home environment.

OPPOSITE: *Although nature has been depicted in the stained glass windows of churches and cathedrals for centuries, not until the advent of the Art Nouveau movement did stained glass become truly organic. Clearly this design does not try to copy nature, but rather creates its own interpretation. This distinction marks the difference between Art Nouveau and that which came before.*

RIGHT: *This stained glass window in gold tones lends a nice dimension to a foyer. The organic designs on the upper and lower panels make for a dramatic entrance indeed. The elaborate wood carving around the window and door is finely wrought— clearly the handiwork of a master craftsman. The carving around the higher windows echoes the shapes in the glass.*

ABOVE: *Art Nouveau designs often present amusing juxtapositions. Take this stained glass window, for example: when it is left open, the building in the distance fills in for the missing glass panel and produces an unintentional trompe l'oeil. The window itself is quite evocative in its own right, from the shape of the upper and lower parts, to the colors and design of the glass panes.*

RIGHT: *Stained glass windows achieved new prominence during the Art Nouveau movement. Today these leaded glass panels can be installed in just about any setting to brighten and inspire the decor. With sunlight pouring through, the panels explode with color and bring a distinctive sense of geometry to any space.*

LEFT: *Louis Tiffany was the greatest practitioner of the stained glass art form, and he inspired a whole generation of artisans. Today stained glass can be used just about anywhere. It can be placed in windows or installed as a partition between rooms, or it can be backlit and hung on a wall.*

ABOVE: *In their attempt to unify the decorative arts, Art Nouveau designers worked in many different mediums. Stained glass was often used to decorate houses inside and out, and ceramic tiles were also implemented in various new ways. As this fancy doorplate and window latch suggest, ironmongery became highly decorative as well. The semi-coffered plaster has a classical motif.*

OPPOSITE: *The salon of this wonderfully designed apartment building demonstrates the meticulous and painstaking detail involved in Art Nouveau architecture. Everything from the floral lighting fixtures and serpentine window mullions to the Modernist furniture and cross-hatch parquet floor was designed by the master himself, Gaudí.*

OPPOSITE: *A vaulted glass ceiling supported by slender iron piers makes this a spectacular space. Besides the tremendous amount of light this ceiling provides during the day, its towering height and intricate, fluid design make a strong impression even at night. The walls are stenciled with the same floral motif as the glass, and the banister and lighting fixtures are just as flamboyantly organic.*

LEFT: *Art Nouveau architecture calls for enormous amounts of time and resources. This stairwell gives a sense of the size of such projects. Imagine the amount of meticulously sculpted iron and carved wood needed to complete even the balustrade that runs along this staircase—not to mention the time required to create the ornate stenciling that graces the walls.*

RIGHT: *A detail of a banister along a Victor Horta staircase shows the tremendous care and craftsmanship involved in the best Art Nouveau design. The wooden spans of the banister are intertwined in a sensual embrace. The intricate wrought-iron grillwork meets the railing seamlessly. The wood, of course, is of the highest quality, buffed and polished to reveal its organic texture.*

RIGHT: *A broad, sweeping staircase can lend a remarkable sense of grandeur to a foyer. These steps rise slowly and elegantly, suggesting a melodic rhythm of line and space that is alluded to throughout the house. The soft lighting adds to the soothing appeal of the space. The coffered ceiling has idiosyncratic iron detailing and is a remarkable piece of Art Nouveau craftsmanship.*

RIGHT: *William Morris was a crucial player in the development of the Art Nouveau movement. Morris was a naturalist whose textile designs were renowned for their beauty as well as their faithful depictions of nature. These embroidered bed linens are excellent examples. The colorful and richly textured designs had a great influence on turn-of-the-century artisans.*

LEFT: *Morris designed some of the world's richest and most luxurious textiles. His wallpaper patterns look fresh and contemporary even today, and they can be used in almost any room setting. In this vignette from Morris's home, the wallpaper was actually designed to tie in with the painting. The simple gilt frame goes perfectly with the rather complex design.*

RIGHT: *This classic Art Nouveau fireplace is appealing for its rich textures and highly articulated symmetry. The coarse, matte finish of the stone mosaic contrasts vividly with the polished tile medallions and the dull luster of the fire irons. The square hearth mouth is small and understated, balanced by the picturesque row of tiles above and the fire irons to each side.*

RIGHT: *The influence of Frank Lloyd Wright is evident in this kitchen's clean, rectilinear shapes and fully integrated design scheme. Wright was one of the innovators of American Art Nouveau, which emphasized a rational, holistic approach to design. The simple elegance and integrity of the table and straight-backed chairs are also reflected in the ceiling beams which are minimally decorated with a diamond cutout motif.*

ABOVE: *This foyer is graced with two fabulous stained glass windows.*
Besides offering a great deal of natural light during the day, the colorful
shapes lend the space another dimension altogether. The window designs
accent the carved panels of the door as well as the iron grate in the window,
giving the room a finished look.

RIGHT: *Victor Horta created some of the world's most fantastic and bizarre architecture. The overall effect of Horta's designs—this living room is one— can be unsettling, yet at the same time beautiful and captivating. This room's tiled ceiling, stained glass entrance, and ornately carved woodwork are typical of Art Nouveau and demonstrate the designer's meticulous attention to detail.*

ABOVE: *The Art Nouveau style attempted to liberate pure visual appeal from the restraint of meaning. Within that context, the autonomous curve was born and became a completely independent decorative ornament. Floral motifs, as well as arabesque and whiplash lines, were employed to impart a dynamic sense of rhythm on the front door of this home.*

ABOVE: *In Vienna and across Eastern Europe, gold became a favorite material of Art Nouveau artists and architects alike. Stenciled gilt foliage was a common ornament on the façades of homes and civic buildings. The technique gives buildings a wonderful luster in daylight. At night, spotlights can be used to great effect as well.*

RIGHT: *A tiled balcony offers a new interpretation of Art Nouveau design. Both the tiles and the iron railing employ a floral motif that is expressed quite differently in the two materials. The contrast makes the design even more dynamic. Architectural symmetry is a key element here.*

ABOVE: *This bedroom corner vignette was designed by Charles Rennie Mackintosh (1868–1928), a master of Art Nouveau. There are few furnishings and the overall decor is quite minimal. Although organic motifs do occur on the stenciled walls, the design is more about the fluid arrangement of line and space.*

OPPOSITE: *Art Nouveau designs can be remarkably ornate, but are just as often remarkably simple. The design of this room is enhanced by its sparse furnishings, which emphasize the exquisite details of the glass-panel walls and other architectural motifs. This room plays on Art Nouveau's linear tendency. The geometry of the room is so precisely designed, in fact, that the rug's grid pattern perfectly complements the lighting fixtures.*

RIGHT: *Charles Rennie Mackintosh had a particularly profound and lasting effect on window design. The way he framed each pane of glass in his windows is remarkable. Mackintosh used glass like a canvas on which to arrange his beautiful and intricate steel mullions. As these windows demonstrate, the geometric designs within the windows transform not only the exterior but also the interior of the building.*

ABOVE: *The most striking features of this dining room and porch are the highly stylized archways. Various elements of the arches come together fluidly and present a remarkable linear rhythm. The succulent blond wood flows harmoniously with the leaded glass panels and the slender iron piers as well. A few plants and a serpentine candelabra echo the curvaceous architecture nicely.*

LEFT: *The autonomous curve is a prevailing motif of Art Nouveau design. Here a swirl of whiplash curves commands a dining room wall, lending the space an oceanic quality. The marble wall tiles complement the window hanging, which resembles a Tiffany stained glass panel in its colorful luminosity. Accessories indicative of the period, a stemlike vase and a feminine statuette, adorn the window ledge.*

CHAPTER THREE

FURNITURE

A few select pieces of Art Nouveau furniture can quickly and dramatically transform a contemporary room. Most Art Nouveau furniture is so inventive that it looks fresh and new—not at all dated—even a century later. Both traditional and modern settings can, therefore, accommodate these pieces. Art Nouveau furnishings can be easily found in antique shops or even at yard sales, and they have a remarkable ability to seduce the adventurous shopper. The style is so unique and intriguing that an Art Nouveau piece will surely become the focus of any room.

It is important to remember, however, that the holistic nature of Art Nouveau design demands a certain degree of cohesiveness in a room. It's a good idea, therefore, to invest in a few other Art Nouveau accessories to make a good piece of furniture look right at home. A Gustav Klimt print or William Morris–inspired carpet, for example, are easy ways to unify a room's Art Nouveau elements.

Keep in mind that Art Nouveau furniture design has two very distinct tendencies—one is "cerebral," while the other is "emotional." The work of Louis Majorelle is a good example of the latter. Majorelle (1859–1929) was one of the most imaginative furniture designers of the Art Nouveau movement. His skill and craftsmanship were just as extraordinary. Raised in the town of Nancy, France,

Majorelle used floral motifs in such a splendid way that he seemed to wholly reinvent furniture and how to use it. A Majorelle chair was as much a lattice for the twisting vines and flowers of his imagination as it was a thing on which to sit. While the traditional shapes of French furniture design were still employed, Majorelle used them in a totally new way. His work often made use of the cabriolet leg, for example, but his fluid organic forms hardly resemble those of his predecessors.

Even in iron and bronze, Majorelle's work has a sense of movement and organic life, of lightness and delicacy. Rushing water and cascading hair are recurring themes that would seem to have little to do with furniture design, but Majorelle renders these motifs so exquisitely that they make perfect sense. In Majorelle's work, one senses that the linear decoration of an object dictates its form, suggesting that—even

OPPOSITE: *A few Art Nouveau furnishings can be used to complement other period pieces. Here, a bow-armed chair brings a touch of levity to a rather ponderous study lined with older antiques. The Art Nouveau cupboard is inlaid with colorful porcelain tiles that also serve to brighten the room.*

in the utilitarian realm of furniture design—Art Nouveau master craftsmen were able to achieve "pure" design.

While just as imaginative, the work of Charles Rennie Mackintosh and the other members of the Glasgow School in Scotland represents Art Nouveau's other, more cerebral, tendency. Far removed from Art Nouveau's decadent, sensual style of floreated abstractions, the Glasgow School was all about order and refinement. The simplicity of line and clarity of purpose that mark Mackintosh's furniture designs rank him among the outstanding artists of the Art Nouveau style.

A perfect example, the Mackintosh chair (see page 65) functions in rigid linear terms rather than flowing organic ones. This architectural design theory was applied to all the arts, and is perhaps most clearly portrayed in furniture. The notion of organic rhythms is still an important element of Art Nouveau design, but in some instances, rectilinear shapes and geometrical curves supersede the whiplash and the arabesque.

RIGHT: *This armchair is well dressed in floral-print upholstery, which suits not only the design of the chair, but also the pattern of the wallpaper. The adjacent table, as well as the carefully planned accessories that adorn it, complement the patterns. Designing all the elements of an interior to produce a harmonious and coherent space is, of course, the ultimate goal of Art Nouveau design.*

LEFT: *This dining room setting brings together a wonderful collection of Art Nouveau furnishings and accessories. The bronze overhead light is perhaps the most striking piece. Its decorative fern leaves and palm fronds extend to four tinted glass shades. Across the room, the side chair's back slats are lyrically carved in the shape of delicate reeds. The cupboard houses an array of beautiful Art Nouveau silver and glassware.*

ABOVE: *In this living room, there is a profound sense of unity and cohesiveness: a simple, highly stylized grid motif brings together the disparate elements of the room. The flat square patterns of the window panes and fireplace tiles are reflected in three dimensions by the lighting fixtures and hearth. The chairs perfectly finish the space, creating a sense of symmetry with the fireplace and windows.*

LEFT: *In its many renditions, the Mackintosh chair has a wonderful sense of simplicity and purity. In a bedroom setting, sheer, diaphanous curtains play nicely against the chair's rigid geometry. With Mackintosh's highly refined furniture designs, a minimalist decor works best.*

ABOVE: *The influence of the Art Nouveau movement is apparent in the sweeping, undulating lines of this sofa. As this example demonstrates, the curvilinear forms of even one Art Nouveau furnishing can completely transform a room.*

OPPOSITE: *Art Nouveau artists favored leaded glass panels for windows, interior doorways, foyers, or any architectural space in the home. Here, stained glass panels accent the fireplace doors, which perfectly suit the carved mantel. The smooth curvilinear shape of the white marble sculpture conveys the essence of the Art Nouveau movement—a purely decorative art form without formal constraints. The clean, sleek design of the straight-back chair reflects the architectonic qualities innovated by Charles Mackintosh and the Glasgow school. The frowning headrest attests to the designer's sense of fun and imbues the chair with a personality of its own.*

RIGHT: *This piece is really quite extraordinary. The design wholly subverts the traditional notion of the hearth and mantel and, in the process, invents a new piece of furniture. The cabinet hearth, so to speak, has a beautifully articulated shape. The fireplace is fully integrated into the design. The ornamental brass plates along the edge of the fireplace complement the cabinet's detailed wood carving.*

The beauty of this cabinet lies in its craftsmanship. The shelves and drawers are meticulously decorated with carvings and various inlaid veneers. The gaggle of geese depicted on the front as well as the goose-head drawer clasps suggest the designer's sense of humor. The silver candelabra and vase on the top shelf are among the array of splendid art objects.

LEFT: *Art Nouveau architecture is remarkable for its fully integrated interiors. Every furnishing in this Art Nouveau living room has been individually crafted to complement the space. Even the carpets, doors, and windows adhere to the highly developed geometry.*

ABOVE: *This bed and side table represent a pinnacle of Art Nouveau design. The floral motifs are lightly and tastefully arranged, and great care has been taken to achieve the bed's fluid lines. The craftsmanship is clearly of the highest degree and the blond wood radiates a sumptuous glow.*

LEFT: *Art Nouveau attempted to bring all of the arts together to create a sense of unity, and nature played a great role in the style's motifs. Here, a finely carved hutch with a forest theme displays plant-like vases. The wallpaper in the background is inspired by a William Morris print.*

ABOVE: *This magnificent bed fits right into its country setting. Its floral ornamentation seems to mirror the abundant foliage seen through the windows. This is a rugged, rustic room that brings the outside in. The bed suits the room perfectly because it is, in essence, a celebration of nature, which Art Nouveau designers revered.*

LEFT: *Art Nouveau designs often assimilate previous styles in a wholly unique context. This fireplace console is a perfect example, bringing Chippendale motifs together with more organic design features. The craftsmanship is of the highest calibre, demonstrated by finrly crenelated latticework around the shelves and a wonderfully embellished crown.*

OPPOSITE: *Judging from the outside of his buildings, it's not surprising that Antonio Gaudí's interiors can seem a bit cavernous. The design of this foyer is quite intriguing, nevertheless, and the furnishings are nothing if not unique. It's not very often, for example, that one sees an upholstered settee with mirror and side table attached.*

CHAPTER FOUR

OBJETS D'ART AND ACCESSORIES

The easiest and least expensive way to convey Art Nouveau style is by incorporating a few art objects into a room's decor. Because of the ornate and effusive quality of Art Nouveau, even a single small item can have a big impact. Objects such as vases, bowls, candlesticks, lamps, and statuettes are quite common and can greatly affect how a room looks and feels. In fact, Art Nouveau's design legacy is perhaps most evident in the applied arts. Advances in silver, china, and glass production were among the greatest achievements of the style.

One doesn't have to be a major collector of Art Nouveau objects to use them effectively in home decorating. A single glass vase can lend just the right touch of color to a room. Similarly, a sinuous, twisting silver candelabra can bring in a subtle note of whimsy. This is where decorating with Art Nouveau becomes really fun. Art Nouveau art objects and accessories often convey such enormous personality that they will become the centerpiece of a room.

A few designers stand out and should be recognized by those who wish to begin collecting Art Nouveau objets d'art. One of them is certainly Louis Comfort Tiffany (1848–1933). Tiffany's glassware is characterized by its swirling rhythmic vitality and opalescence. In 1880 Tiffany patented Favrile glassware, a type of handmade iridescent glass produced by exposing hot glass to a series of metallic fumes and oxides. Through Tiffany, this glass became as much a trademark of Art Nouveau as the whiplash curve. By the turn of the century, glass firms across Europe and North America were trying cheap methods of producing iridescent glass, but none could compare to Tiffany's in terms of color, imagination, or craftsmanship. Some of Tiffany's most inventive designs were his metalwork lamps, in which glass and bronze were sculpted together to form objects of unbelievable fantasy.

The first great exponent of Art Nouveau in France was Emile Gallé (1846–1904) of Nancy. A botanist by training, his glassware did more to advance the botanical aspect of Art Nouveau than any other single factor. Gallé's work demonstrates a particularly successful marriage of elements drawn from Rococo and Oriental art with those of Art Nouveau itself. Although his glassware never became as wild and

OPPOSITE: *Lighting fixtures received special attention during the Art Nouveau period. Since the light bulb had been invented in the late nineteenth century, Art Nouveau designers were really the first to realize the vast artistic potential of lighting fixtures. More often than not these fixtures assume wild, organic shapes and have intricate glass shades.*

free-flowing as Tiffany's, his shapes were often strange and fantastic. Gallé was too much of a naturalist to go as far in abstraction as Tiffany. Instead, he gave Impressionistic versions of various species of flowers delineated faithfully in strong, opalescent colors.

Besides being the first to refer to "un art nouveau" in writing, Henri Van de Velde (1863–1957) was also one of the most important artisans of the movement. A painter by trade, the Belgian Van de Velde eventually worked in almost the whole range of applied arts, including bookbinding, posters, furniture, lighting, cutlery, and even kitchenware. Van de Velde was a follower of William Morris, and his designs reflect the same aesthetic and moral convictions. Like Morris, Van de Velde believed that art should be a source of pleasure for everyone, rich and poor, day in and day out. He wanted to make art for common people as a means of social reformation. Although Van de Velde's architecture gained him his first acclaim and is certainly remarkable, he is most readily identified with his work in the applied arts.

BELOW: *Although these ballroom lights were designed at the turn of the century, they seem modern even by today's standards. The fine craftsmanship and integrity of construction, however, give away the fixtures' Art Nouveau pedigree and lend the room a glamorous, old-word ambience.*

ABOVE: *Art Nouveau lighting fixtures can be used in just about any setting to bring a sense of levity. Here, an Art Nouveau standing floor lamp greatly enhances an otherwise austere study. The lamp's vine-like base and floral, curlicue glass top complement the room's more rigid, rectilinear shapes.*

ABOVE: *As pretty and fresh as a posy of buttercups, this bronze lamp radiates springtime all year round. The lamp gives off a nice ambient glow, but it is just as fun to admire in broad daylight. The design is quite precious, right down to the mushroom pods at the lamp's base. The delicate flower stalks seem almost to be blowing in the breeze.*

RIGHT: *A finely woven silk lamp shade casts a soft, warm glow and can alter the ambience of a room considerably. This practice was inspired by Eastern textiles, which became quite popular in Western Europe at the turn of the century and greatly influenced Art Nouveau artisans.*

LEFT: *The female form became a favorite motif of Art Nouveau painting and sculpture. The figure was often quite abstracted and was even integrated into floral or other organic forms. As in other Art Nouveau mediums, sculptures can be identified by their dynamic, curvaceous forms. This female bust seems to compose itself right out of the earth.*

ABOVE: *A few Art Nouveau pieces can go a long way. These two andirons are a perfect example. Their curious design lends just the right touch to a cozy living room setting. A spare, minimalist decor can afford only a few such ornate pieces before seeming overdone.*

OPPOSITE: *This bedroom features two Tiffany lamps coupled with two Art Nouveau armchairs and an occasional table. The pieces do not appear dated at all, and in fact the room feels quite contemporary despite its Art Nouveau accessories. An opalescent vase shaped like a blooming flower rests on the table.*

RIGHT: *This colorful Art Nouveau melange is exceptional for the quality and variety of the individual pieces. The table lamp and Favrile glass vase on the coffee table suggest Louis Tiffany's great powers of color. The torchére is exquisitely rendered as well. Indeed, the lamp's delicate tendrils seem to creep and slither along before your very eyes. The whole room is like an Art Nouveau fantasy world.*

BELOW: *For Art Nouveau designers, lighting fixtures were a new means of creative expression that allowed them to show off their craftsmanship in various luminous materials. This rather architectonic wall sconce weds stained glass with wrought iron.*

ABOVE: *Painted in warm, moody colors, this Tiffany lamp casts an evocative light on several other fine Art Nouveau pieces. The slender brass candlestick is noteworthy for its intriguing shape. The base forms a whirling S-curve, while the fluted stem features a delicate clasp. The vase painted with a woman's image and the ashtray are both indicative of Art Nouveau, as is the ornate "bouquet of flowers" embedded in the table.*

ABOVE: *The fancifulness of this doorplate suggests the extravagance of Art Nouveau design. It is remarkable that such small details were even considered, much less executed with such fine and laborious craftsmanship. Similarly, the candlesticks are other small but significant considerations: the simple, sturdy iron construction is greatly enhanced by unique, attractive handles.*

OPPOSITE: *A room can have a modern decor and still include an Art Nouveau touch. In fact, most Art Nouveau pieces look more modern than today's contemporary pieces do. This brass hearth screen, for example, is an excellent addition to this rather polished contemporary setting. The screen's curvilinear design complements the room's classical decor nicely.*

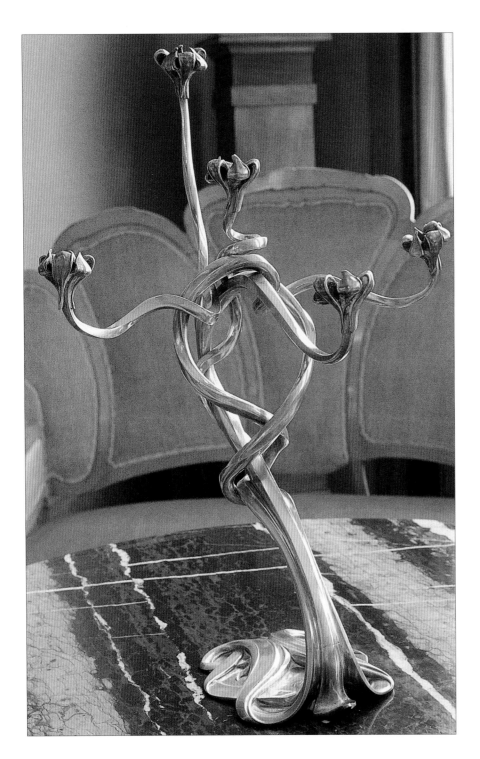

LEFT: *This silver candelabra is a paragon of Art Nouveau design. The floral motif and curvilinear shape could not be more pronounced. The silver is finely wrought and the details are extremely well articulated. While the fine craftsmanship makes the piece appropriate for the most formal settings, its bohemian qualities help it fit into more casual settings as well.*

OPPOSITE: *An extraordinary example of Art Nouveau craftsmanship, this copper mantelpiece features embossed floral motifs and whiplash curves on the front of the mantel, which has been burnished and highly polished. Simple and well crafted, the copper and brass bowl and brass candlesticks are perfect accessories because they do not take away from the mantelpiece itself. The hammered copper frame around the Renaissance-style painting ties the vignette together.*

RIGHT: *Louis Tiffany's Favrile glassware is characterized by opalescence and an organic, abstract quality. Tiffany's iridescent glass became as much a trademark of Art Nouveau as the whiplash curve. Emile Gallé's glassware, on the other hand, is more botanical in nature, although his vases also become exaggerated into strange, fantastic shapes. Together, Tiffany and Gallé produced the most evocative glassware the world has known and have inspired artisans for generations to mimic their work.*

LEFT: *This collection of objets d'art demonstrates just how diverse the Art Nouveau style can be. The polychrome glass vase has an intriguing shape and a transcendent blue-green hue. The candlesticks share the vase's sinewy composition, although they are much more elongated. The clock's architectonic quality suggests the holistic nature of Art Nouveau design.*

ABOVE: *The details of this door are exquisite. Close inspection of the leaded glass panels shows the complexity of the design. The woodwork, too, is subtly carved and precisely indented. The brass handles, however, steal the show. Not only is their shape unique and inspired, but the craftsmanship is equally superb. The slender arms swirl into their base with elegance and grace.*

ABOVE: *One of the easiest ways to imbue one's home with the flavor of Art Nouveau is through posters and prints. Poster art became a popular means of expression during the Art Nouveau period, and even today originals are fairly easy to find. They are interesting not only for their colors and beautiful design, but also for the intriguing way in which printed text is artfully woven into the picture.*